LIVING *the* PRAYER *of* JESUS

LIVING *the* PRAYER *of* JESUS

A Study of the Lord's Prayer in Aramaic

Stephanie Rutt

RESOURCE *Publications* · Eugene, Oregon

LIVING THE PRAYER OF JESUS
A Study of the Lord's Prayer in Aramaic

Copyright © 2019 Stephanie Rutt. All rights reserved. Except for brief quotations in critical publications or reviews, no part of this book may be reproduced in any manner without prior written permission from the publisher. Write: Permissions, Wipf and Stock Publishers, 199 W. 8th Ave., Suite 3, Eugene, OR 97401.

Resource Publications
An Imprint of Wipf and Stock Publishers
199 W. 8th Ave., Suite 3
Eugene, OR 97401

www.wipfandstock.com

PAPERBACK ISBN: 978-1-5326-7020-6
HARDCOVER ISBN: 978-1-5326-7021-3
EBOOK ISBN: 978-1-5326-7022-0

Manufactured in the U.S.A. OCTOBER 22, 2019

Scripture quotations from The Authorized (King James) Version. Rights in the Authorized Version in the United Kingdom are vested in the Crown. Reproduced by permission of the Crown's patentee, Cambridge University Press

For all those who seek the Christ

Contents

Preface | ix

Acknowledgments | xi

The Lord's Prayer: *Authorized (King James) Version and Aramaic Translations* | xiii

The Lord's Prayer: *General Aramaic Interpretations with Transliteration* | xv

Introduction: *Lord, teach us to pray . . .* | xix

Our Father which art in heaven | 1

Hallowed be thy name | 7

Thy kingdom come | 12

Thy will be done | 17

In earth, as it is in heaven | 17

Give us this day our daily bread | 24

And forgive us our debts | 29

As we forgive our debtors | 29

And lead us not into temptation | 34

But deliver us from evil | 34

For thine is the kingdom and the power, and the glory forever. Amen. | 40

Conclusion | 45

How the Lord's Prayer *Informs Our Understanding of the Cross* | 47

Sampling of Participants' Lord's Prayers | 50

Bibliography | 65

Preface

I WAS A BIT nervous as I drove into the parking lot that morning. A Catholic retreat center had invited me to come and present a daylong workshop on the Our Father, the Lord's Prayer, in Aramaic, using my recently published book. By that time, I had given courses, as well as workshops and presentations, on the prayer. But this was a different audience—nuns as well as Catholic lay people, and I, an interfaith minister, was feeling a bit squeamish in presuming to inform them, in any way, in regards to their beloved Our Father.

Ah, but I had momentarily forgotten the power of the Aramaic language and how, like a laser, it can cut through all of our, sometimes, rote and repetitious practices of the prayer to suddenly, and unceremoniously, leave us *besieged* by love everlasting (ref. Ps 139). Indeed, I had momentarily forgotten that, in such moments, we instantly know what St. Augustine meant when he said, "If you have understood, it is not God."[1]

So, during my time with the Sisters and others devoted to the Our Father, I did offer some explanation about the expanded meanings revealed through the Aramaic language but, mostly, I invited them into the experience of their beloved Our Father through the language itself with chant and simple circle liturgical movement. By our lunch

1. Augustine, sermon 117.5, quoted in Johnson, *Quest for the Living God*, 13.

break, one of the nuns said, "You've got my attention!" And, by the end of the day, a lovely bright-faced nun said simply, "I'm taking your CD [compact disc] and learning the prayer in Aramaic. I've been saying and leading the Our Father every day for over thirty-five years. I will never say it the same way again."[2]

Over the years since, I've heard the same sentiment expressed again and again from devout Christians such as the Sisters, to those devoted to other faith traditions, and from many simply identifying as spiritual but not religious. The Aramaic language, engaging the depth of Jesus' message in teaching us how to pray, leaves us silent—heads bowed and hearts opened, pulsing with that love everlasting.

You can view me saying the prayer in Aramaic, using simple arm gestures I've cultivated over the years, on my website at https://www.stephanierutt.com/teaching-sharings-services.html. You can also find teaching audio files there to learn the Aramaic pronunciations at your own pace (https://www.stephanierutt.com/the-lords-prayer.html).

Welcome to the journey. It will not leave you where you began.

God bless!

Rev. Dr. Stephanie Rutt

---

2. Workshop was held at Our Lady of Hope, House of Prayer, New Ipswich, New Hampshire, 2013.

Acknowledgments

MY DEEPEST GRATITUDE IS extended to Neil Douglas-Klotz, author of *Prayers of the Cosmos: Meditations on the Aramaic Words of Jesus*, and to Rocco A. Errico, author of *Setting a Trap for God: The Aramaic Prayer of Jesus*, for providing permission to reference their respective Aramaic translations of the Lord's Prayer. While readers will notice varying nuances between the translations, it is affirming to know that the core meanings for each line of the prayer remain consistent between these two well-known Aramaic scholars.

The Lord's Prayer: *Authorized (King James) Version and Aramaic Translations*

King James Biblical Translation	Aramaic Translation
Our Father which art in heaven,	Abwoon d'bwashmaya,
Hallowed be thy name.	Nethqadash shmakh.
Thy kingdom come.	Teytey malkuthakh.
Thy will be done	Nehwey tzevyanach aykanna
in earth, as it is in heaven.	d'bwashmaya, aph b'arha.
Give us this day our daily bread.	Hawvlan lachma d'sunqanan yaomana.
And forgive us our debts (trespasses),	Washboqlan khaubayn (wakhtahayn),
as we forgive our debtors (those who trespass against us).	aykanna daph khnan shbwoqan l'khayyabayn.
And lead us not into temptation,	Wela tahlan l'nesyuna,
but deliver us from evil:	ela patzan min bisha:
For thine is the kingdom,	Metol dilakhie malkuthakh,
and the power, and the glory,	wahayla, wateshbukhta,
forever.	l'ahlam almin.
Amen.	Ameyn.

Setting a trap for God is the ancient meaning of prayer.
And, it suggests that we can trap all the
love, joy, truth, peace, energy, and compassion we need
when we are receptive to all which is rightly ours.

—ROCCO A. ERRICO[1]

---

1. Errico, *Setting a Trap*, 7.

The Lord's Prayer: *General Aramaic Interpretations with Transliteration*[1]

Bold = Accent; *Italics = Slight Guttural Sound*

General Aramaic Interpretations in Bold Italics	*Aramaic Transliterations in Parentheses*
Our Father which art in heaven,	Abwoon d'bwashmaya,
Remember . . .	(Ah b**woon** deh'baush **maya**)
Hallowed be thy name.	Nethqadash shmakh.
Create Space . . .	(net **kau** dish shm*uck*)
Thy kingdom come.	Teytey malkuthakh.
Align with the Creator . . .	(taa taa **maul** koo *tah*)
Thy will be done	Nehwey tzevyanach aykanna
Manifest the Vision . . .	(*ne*whay se bee **ya***na* ikana)
in earth, as it is in heaven.	d'bwashmaya, aph b'arha.
Become Heaven on Earth . . .	(deh'baush **maya off** bah'are **ahhhh**)

1. The *General Aramaic Interpretations in Bold Italics* have been derived from my years of study of the prayer and will follow throughout the book. The *Aramaic Transliterations in Parentheses* are offered to aid in pronunciation.

GENERAL ARAMAIC INTERPRETATIONS WITH TRANSLITERATION

Give us this day our daily bread. *Embrace Fullness . . .*	Hawvlan lachma d'sunqanan yaomana. (**hauv** laun **lock** mah d'soon kau nan yah oh **ma**na)
And forgive us our debts (trespasses), *Forgive Self . . .*	Washboqlan khaubayn (wakhtahayn), (**wash** bah **claun** *how* **bain** *walk* tau **hain**)
as we forgive our debtors (trespassers) *Forgive Others . . .*	aykanna daph khnan shbwoqan l'khayyabayn. (**ikana** *duf* **kahnan** *shwa* kau nal' **hi** ya bain)
And lead us not into temptation, *Resist Forgetfulness . . .*	Wela tahlan l'nesyuna, (**way lah** *tau* laun **leh'**neh **su**na)
but deliver us from evil: *Cultivate Harmony . . .*	ela patzan min bisha: (**aa** lah patzan men **bee** sha)
For thine is the kingdom, *For Thine is the Vision . . .*	Metol dilakhie malkuthakh, (meh tool deh **lahk** hay **maul** koo *tah*)
and the power, and the glory, *the Energy . . . and the Song . . .*	wahayla, wateshbukhta, (*wah* **hi** lah wah tesh ***book*** tah)
forever. *forever.*	l'ahlam almin. (l'ah**laum** al**mean**)
Amen. *Amen.*	Ameyn. (ah **main**)

I hope and pray that many inspired translations may occur—
in both the transformed words and the actions of those
who confront the Cosmic Christ
through the words of the Aramaic Jesus.[2]

—NEIL DOUGLAS-KLOTZ

2. Douglas-Klotz, *Prayers of the Cosmos*, 8.

Introduction: Lord, teach us to pray . . .

LET'S GO BACK TOGETHER. Before there was anything called Christianity; before the nativity story; before the crucifixion or resurrection. Let's go back in our mind's eye and imagine what, very likely, was quite an ordinary-looking young man. This one called Jesus. A Jew from Nazareth. A humble carpenter who enjoyed no special status in the community. A teacher, for those who would hear, who would only teach for three short years. And yet, it was *through the experience* of this seemingly quite ordinary being, that those who did hear and were able to receive would carry and transmit the message from one generation to the next, birthing what would eventually come to be called Christianity.

This *through the experience* of his being is central. In *The Sins of Scripture*, John Shelby Spong writes, "Christianity began when people had a life-changing experience that was associated with the one named Jesus of Nazareth. That experience, which called them beyond their boundaries into new dimensions of humanity, was accompanied by feelings of wonder, awe and wholeness. Yet, that experience as yet had no shape or form. The best they could do at the beginning to put their experience into words was to utter an ecstatic cry."[1]

1. Spong, *Sins of Scripture*, 221.

INTRODUCTION: LORD, TEACH US TO PRAY...

"To utter an ecstatic cry." Christianity was born of an *experience!* And, I would humbly offer that we too can, today, find our way into that same experience. We too can be left silent except for our own involuntary ecstatic cry. And, in such moments, fully attuned with Jesus, the Christ, we too can experience ourselves as the light of the world as Jesus told us we were (see Matt 5:14).

And, how may we do this? One way is through prayer. Imagine with me again, long ago, sitting in nature and feeling a sense of wonder, perhaps even awe, experiencing this one called Jesus and, of course, wanting to hold on to such an awakening. I would imagine it was this desire that prompted one among them to say, *"Lord, teach us to pray"* (Luke 11:1). And, Jesus answered with what we now call the *Lord's Prayer*. Graciously, all we need to know about keeping our own inner ecstatic cry alive is contained in this prayer.

Now perhaps you are asking, as I initially did, how can this be? I grew up with this prayer and, though certainly important, it did not teach me about the ecstatic cry. I would offer that what is missing to illicit such a cry was lost when the prayer was translated from the original Aramaic into subsequent languages such as Greek, Latin, and English. As you will discover in this study, when we examine the words of Jesus through the lens of the language he spoke, Aramaic, not only do new vistas of meaning emerge but, as importantly, an awakening sense of awe is born through the experience of the language itself. My experience has been, along with many others with whom I have been blessed to study, that this prayer, known from memory by many of us for a lifetime, suddenly starts to awaken and inform us in new ways as the Aramaic language permeates our being.

INTRODUCTION: LORD, TEACH US TO PRAY . . .

A more practical look at the prayer also offers important information about how we can keep the ecstatic cry within alive. In the first half of the prayer:

> Our Father which art in heaven,
> Hollowed be thy name.
> Thy kingdom come.
> Thy will be done in earth, as it is in heaven.

Jesus answers with a clear explanation about where to find God, how to keep our connection with our creator alive and the importance of aligning our will to God's will in bringing heaven to earth. The first half of the prayer informs us of our divinity and instructs us on how to be God's instruments. What could bring greater joy? The second half of the prayer:

> Give us this day our daily bread.
> And forgive us our debts (trespasses),
> as we forgive our debtors (those who trespass against us).
> And lead us not into temptation,
> but deliver us from evil:
> For thine is the kingdom, and the power, and the glory, forever.
> Amen

Jesus offers practical instruction on how we are to be with one another. The second half of the prayer informs us of our humanity. Here, we are reminded that all of our needs are met. We are shown why forgiving our self is as important as forgiving others and how we can avoid the temptations that can lead us astray.

Finally, and blessedly, Jesus reminds us that, in moments of awakening, as our divine nature is expressed through our humanity, we, as children of the living God, are poised to become instruments for the kingdom, the power and the glory here on earth. We feel our heartbeat in sync with all creation and, undone, we can do nothing but exclaim our own unchecked ecstatic cry!

Welcome Home.

Abwoon d'bwashmaya
Our Father which art in heaven
Remember . . .

IN RESPONSE TO LORD, *teach us to pray* (see Luke 11:1), Jesus' first words were *Abwoon d'bwashmaya*. Let's examine this phrase through the lens of the Aramaic language.

Aramaic Translations:[1]

Neil Douglas-Klotz:
Abwoon: "derived from the Aramaic word for personal father *abba* . . . its original roots do not specify a gender and could be translated 'divine parent.' . . . the Absolute, the Only Being, the pure Oneness and Unity, source of all power and stability . . . a birthing, a creation, a flow of blessing . . . the breath or spirit that carries this flow, echoing the sound of breathing . . . the vibration of this creative breath from Oneness as it touches and interpenetrates form."[2]

---

1. Douglas-Klotz and Errico offer variations in spelling in their perspective Aramaic translations. For simplification and consistency throughout, I've chosen to use Douglas-Klotz spellings in my commentaries. There is no personal or academic preference intended.

2. Douglas-Klotz, *Prayers of the Cosmos*, 13.

d'bwashmaya: "the root *shm* which may mean light, sound, vibration, name, or word ... indicates that which rises and shines in space."[3]

Summarizing the phrase, he describes *Abwoon* as pointing to the Absolute and *d'washmaya* as pointing to the manifestation of the One through breath, vibration, light and sound.[4]

Rocco A. Errico:

Awoon: *Abba*, the root of *Awoon*, "is the child's word for father, equivalent to the English 'daddy' . . . But precisely because *Abba* imaginatively conjures up childhood feelings of intimacy and dependency, for those who so address God, the immense distance between God and themselves has collapsed."[5] "He instructs his disciples to approach God as Father directly, without intermediaries."[6]

dwashmaya: "who [is] in heaven ... from the Hebrew word *shamayim* ... [Errico explains that brackets are placed around "is" because in the Aramaic text this verb is not present.] can also mean 'sky,' 'universe,' 'cosmos,' and, by implication, 'everywhere.'"[7]

Summarizing the phrase, he writes, "Our Father who [is] throughout the universe," or "Our Father who [is] everywhere."[8]

Let's take a closer look. First of all, the opening sound of the prayer, *A* of *Abwoon*, is pronounced *ahhhh*. This

3. Douglas-Klotz, *Prayers of the Cosmos*, 14.
4. Douglas-Koltz, *Prayers of the Cosmos*, 13–14.
5. Errico, *Setting a Trap*, 28.
6. Errico, *Setting a Trap*, 27.
7. Errico, *Setting a Trap*, 37.
8. Errico, *Setting a Trap*, 37.

primal sound is often uttered when there are no words. It is quite interesting to me that, as you will see, the *Lord's Prayer* begins with this sound, completes the first half of the prayer with this sound, and ends with this same *ahhhh* sound. It makes a circle in both sound and meaning. Jesus was seeding the beginnings of the ecstatic cry within those present by beginning with *ahhhh*.

And, how wonderful that by responding *Abwoon d'bwashmaya*, Jesus was telling all who could hear that this *awe*some God was as close as their breath and could be, for them, as intimate as an earthly father. We can imagine how startling this image of God likely seemed to them as it was far removed from the prevailing notion of God being a deity largely separate from the world of human beings and daily affairs. Yet, at the same time, Jesus was also describing God as Absolute, the source of all power. In today's theological language, this view is reflected beautifully in the new worldview known as panentheism—that is we may truly experience God as *both* immanent *and* transcendent.[9]

Further, it would seem that Jesus was pointing his followers inward, encouraging them to cultivate their own intimate connection with the creator, using the breath as the most visceral vehicle for awakening such an inner connection. And what could be more intimate, more vital, to us than breathing? How do we know we are born? We breathe. How do we know we have passed over? We stop breathing. In the meantime, we could say that we are most intimately connected with our creator through our breath.

I would take this a step further. It is a common belief that we breathe. I would say, instead, that *we are breathed* and that awareness of our breath invites us into the most

9. Artson, "Holy, Holy, Holy!," 20.

intimate and reciprocal relationship with our creator. In fact, one cannot say *ahhhh* without the full exhale born of an inhale. Jesus wanted the disciples to have a visceral experience of the One to whom they belonged. He wanted them to experience *being breathed*.

And with breath there is life and we are born into the image and likeness of our Father. How fitting that Jesus would make what could be quite an unapproachable, esoteric notion of the creator into one that was as familiar and intimate as an earthly father. Are we not also born in the image and likeness of our earthly father and mother? Do we need to ask to be connected to them? No. It is our birthright.

And concluding this opening phrase, *d'bwashmaya*, Douglas-Klotz's notion of the breath, originating from Oneness, interpenetrating our forms, reminds me of the thirteenth-century Christian mystic Meister Ekhart's reminder, "We are all mothers of God."[10] Perhaps with each breath, now intimately connected with our creator, we are poised to birth, bring, to be, heaven on earth. Similarly, Kabir said, "All know that the drop merges into the ocean but few know that the ocean merges into the drop."[11] How wonderful to know that, with full awareness of our breath, we can *remember*, reconnect, with our blessed creator who breathed us into life and who, in fact, is continuously merging with us each moment with each breath. And, in such moments, we intimately and gloriously *experience* our unity with all beyond our unique, individual expression. We begin to recognize that, as flowers of the field, while we are each different, we are all brought forth by the same creator. And, moments of such remembering bring

10. Fox, *Meditations with Meister Eckhart*, 74.
11. Kabir, *Bijak*, 96.

a kind of opening that heals us on many levels inviting rebirth . . . again and again . . . as we are breathed.

Jesus pointed to this in his daily contact with others. Let's look at some examples:

Biblical References:

> Mark 7:32–35: Jesus heals a deaf man who had an impediment to his speech saying, "Eth-pha-tah," meaning *Be opened*.

> John 3:5–8: Jesus tells Nicodemus, "Verily, verily, I say unto thee, Except a man be born of water and of spirit, he cannot enter into the kingdom of God. That which is born of the flesh is flesh; and that which is born of the Spirit is spirit. Marvel not that I say unto thee, Ye must be born again. The wind bloweth where it listeth, and thou hearest the sound thereof, but canst not tell whence it cometh, and whither it goeth: so is every one that is born of the Spirit."

Much like it is the awareness of breath that reconnects us to our unity with all creation, it is the deeper and deeper opening to this breath of life that heals us. Perhaps to be *born again* means that, in each and every moment, with each breath, we can be, blessedly, born again both in the flesh and in the spirit and experience *being* heaven on earth.

In answering the request, *Lord, teach us to pray*, Jesus answered, *Abwoon d'bwashmaya, Our Father which art in heaven*, inviting all to **remember**—remember your beloved God is here, as close as your breath. Tune inward and simply remember. There is nothing to "do." Being your creator's breath is your birthright. Be still and know (see Ps 46:10) that you are intimately connected with your

Father. You are already home, right here, right now, in your Father's heavenly creation.

Questions for Reflection

1. Describe in your own words the *ecstatic cry*. Have you had such an experience?
2. What shift occurs in you when you contemplate *being breathed* instead of simply breathing?
3. What does it say to you that Jesus used the familiar *abba* to refer to God the Father?
4. Given our expanded understanding offered through the study of the Aramaic language, how would you define or describe being *born again?*

Nethqadash shmakh
Hallowed be thy name
Create Space . . .

WITH THE SWEET REMEMBRANCE that *we are breathed*, naturally comes the realization of St. Therese of Lisieux when she declared, "I am the atom of Jesus,"[1] or what is described in the Hindu scripture, the Bhagavad Gita, 9:5, as the greatest of secrets: that God does not so much live in us but, rather, we live in God.[2] With the awareness that there is no separation between us and our creator, we pause in the deep knowing that *we are that which we seek*. I think of the *Abwoon d'bashmaya* as a kind of quick sudden *uhhh!* that instinctively happens when we suddenly remember something we've forgotten. And then as naturally as an exhale follows an inhale, the *Nethqadash shmakh*, brings us inward where this remembrance can begin to deepen our intimate connection with our creator and to, finally, at long last, feed our deepest hunger.

Aramaic Translations:

Neil Douglas-Klotz:
Nethqadash: "holy . . . evokes the images of clearing or sweeping and of preparing the

1. Therese of Lisieux, *Poetry*, 106.
2. Satchidananda, *Living Gita*, 129.

ground for an important plant . . . the inner shrine by which God's name is hallowed can be developed only through letting go, releasing some of the clutter inside that keeps us too busy to be silent and receptive to the 'still, small voice.'"[3]

shmakh: [From] "the root *shm*—the divine name."[4]

Rocco A. Errico:
Nethqadash: "pure, holy, a holy one, or saint . . . comes from the Semitic root verb *qdsh*, 'to be holy, to hallow, to sanctify, to consecrate, to set apart for a specific purpose, to dedicate for a holy use or to a cause.'"[5] "But like the Holy One who has called you, set yourselves apart in your entire manner of living. Because it is written, 'You shall sanctify yourselves and be holy, for I am holy.'"[6] (see 1 Pet 1:15–16)
shmakh: "name"[7]

Hallowed be Thy name. If there is no separation between us and our creator, if we are, in fact, that which we seek, then I would humbly offer that "Thy" name is pointing to each of us as unique manifestations or expressions of our creator, much like those flowers of the field we spoke of earlier. And, just like we each have our own name, I like to think we each have our own unique vibration one could call a note. And, just like all notes make up the song,

---

3. Douglas-Klotz, *Prayers of the Cosmos*, 17.
4. Douglas-Klotz, *Prayers of the Cosmos*, 17.
5. Errico, *Setting a Trap*, 41.
6. Errico, *Setting a Trap*, 44.
7. Errico, *Setting a Trap*, 41.

collectively, "We are one great song from the heart of God," as Dan Schutte exclaims in his song "All One People."[8]

And, what can we imagine becomes important when it lands in our hearts that *we* each are holy expressions of our creator called by a hallowed name? I can imagine that, **remembering**, we suddenly yearn to **create space** to safeguard, set apart, cultivate, nourish that blossoming seed of our inner divinity, to pause and give thanks to our creator for our blessings. Such an image is beautifully captured in the well-known Angelus print by Jean-Francois, showing two peasants in a field bowing over a basket of potatoes saying a prayer. *Nethqadash shmakh* invites us into the full humility of our divine holiness. Again, our head bows and our heart opens. And the following scriptural passages become very real to us.

Biblical References:

> Ps 51:10: "Create in me a pure heart, O God, and renew a right spirit within me."

> 2 Cor 7:1: "Having therefore these promises, dearly beloved, let us cleanse ourselves from all filthiness of the flesh and spirit, perfecting holiness in the fear of God."

> Eph 1:4: "According as he hath chosen us in him before the foundation of the world, that we should be holy and without blame before him in love."

Yet, sometimes nourishing the blossoming seed of our inner divinity is not such an easy task, as it requires us to clear away all that may hinder or restrict that blossoming.

---

8. Schutte, *Drawn by a Dream*, compact disc.

And, it can be difficult to let go, clear away, what may have felt familiar for a very long time. What do we need to let go of in order to hear more clearly in our prayers and meditations? What do we need to cultivate to tenderly nourish the seed of our growing connection with our creator?

It is important to remember that we do not have to create the connection. We just have to tune the channel to hear more clearly. The signal, our divine connection, is already there! *Nethqadash shmakh* points to the importance of setting our focus apart and in a singular fashion so we can hear the call of our creator and respond with humble hearts to bring forth our divine purpose. It challenges us to enter into a deep inner reflection so as to nourish the divine seed within, remembering that the seed already contains all it needs to flourish. We, as trusted caretakers, simply become joyful instruments of a greater good to which we can only attest. For our divine purpose does not come *from* us but, rather, moves *through* us as grace may allow. It is in this way we become an expression of the most holy who breathed us into life.

This is spiritual practice, on and off, our mats. Through prayer and meditation, we clear a space inside for the creator to live, breath, express, and manifest through us. Here we take time out from the busyness of daily life to listen. As Mother Teresa said, "In the silence and purity of the heart God speaks."[9] In such moments, the light of *shem* brings clarity and focus of our innate, unique spark and opens a space for what may be next for us to be revealed.

---

9. Mother Teresa, *In the Heart*, 23.

Questions for Reflection

1. What are some of the ways that you would like to *make holy*?

2. What does the image of "standing over" or "bowing over" the soil we have tenderly cleared for our seed-planting say to you?

3. How would you describe your current spiritual practice if you are currently engaged in one? How does it serve you, challenge you, unfold you, heal you, restore you?

4. What are some of the things you sense need to be cleared away in your inner and outer life in order to *make holy* each moment?

Teytey malkuthakh

Thy kingdom come

Align with the Creator . . .

WHEN WE *REMEMBER* AND *create space* within for listening, the seed of our mutual desire with the One can be planted. Now we are ripe to *align with the creator* who loved us into birth. We now yearn to live our lives from the essence of that holy place within. We begin to yearn to have our will and the divine will be one and the same. We yearn to be good instruments; but to be good instruments, we first must align with our creator. It is only in this way that *Thy kingdom come* can be expressed through us.

Aramaic Translations:

Neil Douglas-Klotz:

Teytey: "come" and also includes images of mutual desire related to the old image of the "nuptial chamber" where mutual desire is fulfilled and birthing begins.[1]

malkuthakh: "a quality of rulership and ruling principles that guides our lives toward unity . . . carries the image of a 'fruitful arm' poised ready to create. . . . It is what says 'I can' within

---

1. Douglas-Klotz, *Prayers of the Cosmos*, 20.

us and is willing, despite all odds, to take a step in a new direction."[2]

Rocco A. Errico:

Taythey: "Let your kingdom come . . . [Jesus] shifted the emphasis away from the usual manner of praying for God's kingdom coming as king . . . the prayer is for a spiritual, social kingdom—a reality that rules from inside the hearts and minds of all human beings."[3]

malkuthakh: "kingdom, derived from the root verb *mlkh* (or *malkh*) and means 'to counsel, to advise'[4] [Translating this phrase]: 'Let divine, spiritual forces (Father's wise counsel or parental loving advice) guide our lives and direct us in all our ways.'"[5]

In this line, we ask that the deepest desires of our heart, our ideas and goals, our unique expression of the kingdom, seeded in us by our creator, be manifest. This is not an intellectual exercise! This is a *very passionate* birthing occurring in the heart—a birthing that integrates two key processes. First, it requires our listening heart both in the silence of our spiritual practice as well as from all the ways the divine is communicating with us through other people, nature, situations and synchronicities. Second, it requires our discerning reflection upon all the ways we put forward and manifest our internal insights, all the ways we take our divine guidance and move it from inner knowing to outer expression.

I call this seed of our mutual desire to align with our creator the *impulse toward wholeness*. It's what births the

2. Douglas-Klotz, *Prayers of the Cosmos*, 20.
3. Errico, *Setting a Trap*, 47–48.
4. Errico, *Setting a Trap*, 48.
5. Errico, *Setting a Trap*, 49.

"*I can!*" in us even when every limb is shaking. It's what gets us out of bed in the morning and quickens our steps. It's what heightens our awareness that there are only so many breaths left. It's what leaves us full of gratitude for each moment. It's what enables us, in spite of all obstacles and challenges, to take a step in a new direction. It's what knows what we are here to do, the gift we carry, the offering we are yearning to share in service to a greater good. It knows, graciously, what we know not. It is the beloved mystery and it yearns *passionately for us!* It's why in the Sacred Hadith Abu Ohar records Allah's assurance, "And whoever comes to me walking, I will go to him running."[6]

But being human, we may question our desire to align with our creator. Most notably, we may question if we have anything of value to offer, if we may be able to bring forth that which is being asked of us, if we have what it takes to birth that which our creator has already seeded within us. Let's look at biblical references that highlight our human insecurities, as well as the mystery that is waiting to be birthed though us, particularly for those times we may feel more like a tiny mustard seed than a towering oak.

Biblical References:

> Exod 3:10: Moses seems to feel this way when the Lord says, "I will send thee unto Pharaoh, that thou mayest bring forth my people the children of Israel out of Egypt."

> Exod 3:11: Moses protests saying, "Who am I?" Is this not how we too feel when confronted with some task we know is going to challenge us or stretch us beyond our comfort zone? This

---

6. Dhar, "110 Hadith Qudsi."

ALIGN WITH THE CREATOR...

is why I love Jesus' description of the kingdom of heaven (remember that's in us!) being like a grain of mustard seed.

Matt 13:31–32: "The kingdom of heaven is like to a grain of mustard seed, which a man took, and sowed in his field: Which indeed is the least of all seed: but when it is grown, it is the greatest among herbs, and becometh a tree, so that the birds of the air come and lodge in the branches thereof."

Contemplate with me for a moment this notion of each of us being like a grain of mustard seed. When we plant a seed in the ground, we know it contains the full blueprint of what it will become. It is our job to clear the space (sound familiar?) and to nourish the seed. With our loving attention, we create the conditions for the seed to grow into the fullest expression of what it can be. Can we offer the same care and loving attention to ourselves? Could it be that our most important job, our most direct way to align with our creator, is to care for the seed of our divinity within us in much the same way we might care for a seedling we plant?

I believe that waiting in the silence of our hearts is the seed which holds the sacred vision our beloved God planted within us at birth for manifestation in our lifetime. It is now our job to till the soil within, to make ripe our listening hearts to receive *what is already there*, the divine's will for our lives. God is there waiting to let us know. It is our job to align, to listen, and then to *act with joyous abandon!*

Questions for Reflection

1. It has been said that it is not our darkness we fear most but, rather, our light. What does this say to you? What has been your experience? What visceral reactions arise when you imagine standing totally powerful, beautiful, and victorious?

2. Often making an important shift, such as stepping into some expression of power which may be new for us, can affect those closest to us and may predispose a change of life circumstance. Sometimes we like things to remain the same for fear of rocking the boat. What has been your experience?

3. Describe a time when you stood strong and firm and free in your *teytey malkuthakh!*

4. Is there a particular counsel or advise you're seeking from God at this point in your life?

Nehwey tzevyanach aykanna
Thy will be done
Manifest the Vision . . .

d'bwashmaya, aph b'arha
in earth, as it is in heaven
Become Heaven on Earth . . .

HAVING **REMEMBERED** TO WHOM we belong, *abwoon d'washmaya*, turned inward to **create space** and cultivate the most holy, *nethqadash shmakh*, and aligned ourselves to receive the sacred vision of the divine's will for us, **teytey malkuthakh**, we are now poised for action to bring heaven to earth or, more importantly, to act in ways that enable us to *become* heaven on earth.

Aramaic Translations:

Neil Douglas-Klotz:
Nehwey: [Thy]
tzevyanach: "'will' but this is not what we usually think of as willpower or trying hard . . . in Aramaic, the word carries the meaning of 'desire' . . . 'heart's desire' that one's goal or purpose

has moved beyond the mental stage. . . . It has become so much a part of oneself that one need no longer think about it."[1]

aykanna: "'just as'. . . the sense of a determined desire toward consistency and stability . . . that God's heart desire be done constantly through our lives."[2]

d'bwashmaya: recall from the first line of the prayer, refers to light, sound, vibration, universe, cosmos.

aph b'arah: "earth . . . points to the feeling, the sigh of the human species, whenever it feels the support of the earth underneath us."[3]

Rocco A. Errico:

Nehweh [Thy]

seweeanah: "will, wish, desire, delight and pleasure . . . the 'will of God' as a father's *good desire* or *pleasure* for his children.[4] . . . It is healthy for us to recognize that God is always *for* us."[5]

akanna: [be] as in "Let your will be"[6]

dwashmaya: In addition to the meanings referenced in the first line of the prayer, he offers the root *shmaya* metaphorically means "peace, harmony, prosperity" and "heaven" as a state of "universal state of peace and harmony" reflective of how the early prophets and wise men observed the planets and other celestial bodies—harmoniously staying in their own orbits and predictable functioning to divine law.

1. Douglas-Klotz, *Prayers of the Cosmos*, 23.
2. Douglas-Klotz, *Prayers of the Cosmos*, 23.
3. Douglas-Klotz, *Prayers of the Cosmos*, 23.
4. Errico, *Setting a Trap*, 59.
5. Errico, *Setting a Trap*, 63.
6. Errico, *Setting a Trap*, 59.

> They concluded that the universe "is order and intelligence."[7]
>
> *ap barah*: "the way, or path . . . the natural laws of the universe are designed for flawless operation. But, when we decide to interfere and break the laws of our being, we move out of our own orbit. We collide with and harm one another and everyone suffers. But by understanding ourselves, and by working with the laws that govern our souls and existence, we can avoid collisions and much unnecessary pain, anguish, and distress."[8]

This line is the fourth and, considered by many, the most central line of the prayer as it is here that heaven meets earth. Here we move away from the solitary safety of the inner world, where we have been remembering, cultivating and aligning, to move outward toward the full manifestation of our vision, God's will for us. And moving toward our creator's desire for us now becomes intrinsic, as natural and as irresistible as breathing—for we know now just who is the "maker and keeper"[9] of our days.

It is now time to act. And it's also a good time to remember that "all things work together for good to them that love God, to them who are called according to his purpose" (Rom 8:28). *All* things work for good. This includes our successes, our so-called failures and triumphs, as well as our struggles and deepest challenges. Each plays an important part in bringing forth God's will for us even if we may not be able to see the purpose or reason at the time. With this profound awareness, born of the experience of unity with our creator and sustained by our deepest faith

---

7. Errico, *Setting a Trap*, 64.

8. Errico, *Setting a Trap*, 65.

9. Farrell, "O God, You Search Me."

and trust, we walk out into our days like a shepherd knowing fully to whom it is we belong.

And, this knowing to whom we belong brings a sweet remembrance that, in good times or bad, all creation is here to support our every move in the creation of our vision, God's will for us! Simply and miraculously, everything we engage through our senses, from our very bodies to the full spectrum of the world around us, is here to support the fruition of our life's divine purpose. I think of this as a big, "Why not?" Why not, indeed, when we are offering every thought, word, and deed to fulfilling a greater good for which we, likely, may only be playing a small part? Yes, indeed, most wondrously, when we align with our creator to simply play our note, our part, in the divine plan, be become humble instruments for *thy will be done, in earth as it is in heaven.*

And, we naturally begin to live as is expressed in the Tao Te Ching by Lao Tzu. "I have just three things to teach: simplicity, patience, compassion . . . simple in actions and in thoughts, you return to the source of your being. Patience with both friends and enemies, you accord with the way things are. Compassion toward yourself, you reconcile all beings in the world."[10] As we remember we are expressions of the living God and have all we need, *Abwoon d'bwashmaya*, our inner and outer lives simplify. As we clear a space for deep listening, *Nethqadash shmakh*, we learn patience in trusting the natural fruition of our divine vision and purpose. And, when we come into full alignment with our creator, becoming instruments of a divine purpose, we are filled with joyful compassion for all beings, *Teytey malkuthakh*, knowing each is also a true

---

10. Mitchell, *Tao Te Ching*, ch. 67.

expression of the one creator. And, in such glorious moments, we are truly poised to bring heaven to earth.

Some beautiful reminders of the reciprocal relationship between heaven and earth and the joy that is created in moments of such unity can be found in Isa 55:10–12:

Biblical References:

> Isa 55:10: "For as the rain cometh down, and the snow from heaven, and returneth not thither, but watereth the earth, and maketh it bring forth and bud, that it may give seed to the sower, and bread to the eater:"

> Isa 55:11: "So shall my word be that goeth forth out of my mouth: it shall not return unto me void, but it shall accomplish that which I please, and it shall prosper in the thing whereto I sent it."

> Isa 55:12: "For ye shall go out with joy, and be led forth with peace: the mountains and the hills shall break forth before you into singing, and all the trees of the field shall clap their hands."

These verses call for a complete letting go of control and a surrendering into the joyous state of being an instrument of grace and beauty, simply here to bring heaven to earth. Yet, it is important to remember that this joy is not a transient emotion. No, graciously, it is a state of joyful devotion that comes from the wellspring within and is not predicated upon outer circumstances or conditions. It is the joy that sustains us when our rudder breaks and we are being tossed about by unforgiving seas. It is the joy that waits at the end of our last prayer when we think all is lost.

And, in the end, it is all that really matters for it is the only thing that can save us.

And so, we rise up in joy to humbly pray to be divine instruments bringing heaven to earth as our creator may direct. And what a bounce it brings to our step when we remember that our beloved God within us, yearning to express through us, is always *for us!* With such divine sponsorship, all we need to bring forth God's vision for our lives, in service to a greater good, is here. Indeed, when we align with our creator to bring forth our unique expression of divinity, all the natural laws of the universe come into harmony to support the manifestation of our Lord's creation through us.

With **remembering**, **creating space**, and **aligning**, we are truly poised to **manifest the vision** and **become heaven on earth**. How fitting that we end the first half of the prayer with *aph B'arha. Ahhhh*, indeed!

Questions for Reflection:

1. Sometimes we think of people as being more inclined toward thinking or doing, visioning or producing. Where do you fall in this spectrum in terms of your comfort level moving from the inner processes to the outer manifestations?

2. As a sower of seed, we practice surrender, yet, we are asking here to manifest our goals or vision in a systematic way in response to our direct alignment with our creator. What does this say to you?

3. We are reassured here that the earth, indeed all the world of the senses, is really a support for us. What has been your experience? Is it a familiar notion to feel supported by your surroundings or not so much

so? If not so much so, what might you do to shift this experience?

We have come to the end of the first half of the prayer. Recall from the introduction, the first half of the prayer informs us of our divinity. Here, Jesus gives a clear explanation of where to find God, *Abwoon d'bashmaya*, how to keep our connection with our creator alive, *Nethqadash shmakh*, and the importance of aligning our will to God's will, *Teytey Malkuthakh*, so his will may be done in bringing heaven to earth through us, *Nehwey tzevyanach aykanna d'bwashmaya aph b'arha*.

Now we are ready to explore the second half of the prayer where Jesus offers practical instruction on how we are to live and be with one another. The second half of the prayer informs us of our humanity.

Hawvlan lachma d'sunqanan yaomana

Give us this day our daily bread

Embrace Fullness . . .

THE SECOND HALF OF the Lord's Prayer focuses on the practical work of cultivating our inner life so we may understand our connection with others more clearly and relate to one another more compassionately. Following on the theme of action just expressed in the previous line of the prayer, here we begin from the ground up or from the inside out. We are pushed and challenged to consider all aspects of our dealings with others and, as we do so, are invited into a deeper experience of wholeness.

Aramaic Translations:

Neil Douglas-Klotz:
Hawvlan: "give . . . humanly generate"[1]
lachma: "both bread and understanding"[2]
d'sunqanan: "refers to needs, but may also mean 'an illuminated measure,' circle of possession,' or nest' . . . points to receiving all we need, sufficient without hoarding."[3]

1. Douglas-Klotz, *Prayers of the Cosmos*, 27.
2. Douglas-Klotz, *Prayers of the Cosmos*, 27.
3. Douglas-Klotz, *Prayers of the Cosmos*, 27.

> *yaomana*: [daily]

Rocco A. Errico:
> [For this line, and continuing through the second half of the prayer, Errico translates each line in its entirety.]
> *Hawlan lahma dsunkana yaumana*: "Provide us our needful bread from day to day."[4]

Errico examines the historical and cultural roots of breaking bread in the Near East and reminds us that there is sacredness in breaking bread together, a bond of trust is formed, representing the bond of sacredness God would want between all of his children.[5] And, inherent in this trust is the faithfulness that "God's presence is ever with us providing whatever is necessary."[6] Symbolically, this line also represents "ideas" and "prosperity" reminding us that God provides us with ideas so that we may prosper and that God's truth gives us an understanding of life, ourselves and others.[7] Indeed, Errico asserts, God is "the Source and the Supply."[8]

Jesus said, "I am the bread of life: he that cometh to me shall never hunger; and he that believeth on me shall never thirst" (John 6:35). When we know to whom we belong, we no longer seek satisfaction from the outer world. We have already been reminded of this in relation to our divine interconnectedness with our creator in the *Abwoon d'bwashmaya*. Here we are reminded of it in relation to our physical needs in our creator's great creation.

---

4. Errico, *Setting a Trap*, 79.
5. Errico, *Setting a Trap*, 80.
6. Errico, *Setting a Trap*, 82.
7. Errico, *Setting a Trap*, 83.
8. Errico, *Setting a Trap*, 85.

This bountiful blessing was foreseen in the beloved Psalm 23, in the first line: "The Lord is my shepherd, I shall not want." The last part of the phrase, "I shall not want," is more succinctly translated, *Lo Echsar*, "I will lack not," or, simply, "I lack not."[9] This clarification offers an important shift in how many commonly understand this line. "I shall not want," orients us toward the future with a directive toward behaviors and outcomes. To "lack not" reminds us of the truth in this present moment—that we are already full! Indeed, if we have been loved into birth by our creator, seeded with a divine purpose, and seek only to make his will our will in bringing heaven to earth, then, of course, it follows that our creator would supply all we need to be his instrument. Allow this profound realization to settle into your bones. *Lo Echsar*. "I lack not." What else could we possibly want or need? And, wondrously, needing nothing we are suddenly free to enjoy all.

And often, as our inner world becomes more, our outer world becomes less. In particular, we find ourselves less drawn to have or hoard more than we need. As Errico writes, "When we hoard money, things, or whatever, we lose them. By hoarding, we block the flow of good *from* us and *to* us."[10] In embracing the notion that *we are already full*, living in interrelational harmony with our creator, we could say that, with each breath, we are engaging the flow of good *from* us in doing beautiful deeds for our creator and *to* us as we receive all we need to accomplish those deeds as instruments in service to a greater good.

The expanded meaning of bread related to our deepening understanding of ourselves and others can, perhaps, most personally, be seen in relation to Douglas-Klotz's

9. Scherman and Zlotwitz, *Tehillim*, 56.

10. Errico, *Setting a Trap*, 86.

"nest," metaphorically personified by our inner community of family and significant others. As we look more closely at this inner community, we see that each has been brought into our lives for a purpose and that each elicits a different response in us. Some delight us, others enrage us. Some are easy to be with, others challenge us to our core. In this light, *our daily bread* offers rich, multi-textured opportunities to mine the treasures, wisdom that can only arise from being in relationship with others. For here, we learn to live Jesus' second commandment in Mark 12:31: "Thou shalt love thy neighbor as thyself." The *as thyself* part becomes important in distilling the boundaries necessary to differentiate our role, part, in our relationships with others. In doing so, we can better receive what nuggets of wisdom are there for us. This is the true work of the *as thyself* part and provides the crucial nourishment for our emotional lives just as forms of physical nourishment sustain our bodies.

And, graciously, in addition to being nourished physically and emotionally, *our daily bread* also includes our spiritual sustenance as we seek to live out the ritual of holy communion in our daily lives: "Jesus took bread, and blessed it, and brake it, and gave it to the disciples, and said, 'Take, eat; this is my body.' And he took the cup, and gave thanks, and gave it to them, saying, 'Drink ye all of it. For this is my blood of the new testament, which is shed for many for the remission of sins'" (Matt 26:26–28). Metaphorically, we could say that Jesus is inviting us to take in the Holy Spirit as we might take in bread, equally vital and necessary to our earthly sustenance. And, in doing so, we receive the balm of the Holy Spirit as our cup overflows.

Let's look as some additional biblical references that speak of bread as spiritual sustenance.

Biblical References:

Luke 4:4: "It is written that man shall not live by bread alone, but by every word of God."

John 6:58: "This is that bread which came down from heaven: not as your fathers did eat manna, and are dead: he that eateth of this bread shall live forever."

Questions for Reflection:

1. Reflect upon the image of "bread" in this line of the prayer. What does the expanded meaning in Aramaic of "practical understanding" say to you?

2. In considering the wisdom gleaned from mining our personal relationships, whom might you invite into your heart in order to better distill the gift being offered to you?

3. Imagine you were participating in Holy Communion in your local parish or church. How might your experience be different as a result of this study?

Washboqlan khaubayn (wakhtahayn)
And forgive us our debts (trespasses)
Forgive Self . . .

aykanna daph khnan shbwoqan l'khayyabayn
as we forgive our debtors (those who trespass against us)
Forgive Others . . .

As we ***embrace fullness*** and are left with only overflowing gratitude, we yearn to better sustain this precious feeling of grace. But, to do so, we must release all the blockages that dam up our ability to receive our creator's full bounty. We must unknot all the ties that bind to release the flow of the Holy Spirit within us. And, this unknotting often requires forgiveness, both of ourselves and others.

It is often said that to forgive is to be set free. That to hold on to angst with another is to actually drink the very poison we think we are giving to the other. As Jack Kornfield, one of the key teachers to introduce the practice of Theravada Buddhism to the West, writes in *A Path with*

Heart, "One ex-prisoner of war said when visiting a fellow survivor, 'Have you forgiven those who imprisoned us yet?' The survivor said, 'No, I haven't. Never.' The first veteran said, 'Then somehow they still have you in prison.'"[1]

Aramaic Translations:

Neil Douglas-Klotz:

Washboqlan: "return to its original state . . . reciprocally absorb . . . reestablish slender ties to . . . and embrace with emptiness."[2]

khaubayn: "'debts' in the Matt version of the prayer and 'sins' *(wakhtahayn)* in the Luke version. . . . From the Aramaic, it could also be rendered as failures, mistakes, accidental offenses, frustrated hopes, or tangled threads."[3]

aykanna: again reminds us (as in the previous *nehwey tzevyanach aykanna*) that releasing must be done consistently and regularly if our knotted relationships are to become whole and stable again.[4]

daph khnan shbwoqan l'khayyabayn: [forgiving others]

Rocco A. Errico:

[As with the previous line, Errico does not translate by word but, rather, offers a commentary on the full line.]

Washwok-lan haubain akana dap hnan shwaqan l'hayawein: "Forgive us our offenses, as we have forgiven our offenders."[5] Also, the

---

1. Kornfield, *Path with Heart*, 280.
2. Douglas-Klotz. *Prayers of the Cosmos*, 31.
3. Douglas-Klotz, *Prayers of the Cosmos*, 31.
4. Douglas-Klotz, *Prayers of the Cosmos*, 31.
5. Errico, *Setting a Trap*, 89.

phrase may be rendered, "Untie or release us [from] our offenses ... *Shwaqan* means forgive, pardon, and also denotes to free, to remit, to untie, to loosen, and to release."[6]

Errico stresses that Jesus knew that forgiveness was the only way to begin the rectification of human mistakes—that blaming doesn't heal but pardoning does. Jesus was well acquainted with the powerful antidote that forgiveness holds for the human heart.[7]

In *Mutant Message from Forever: A Novel of Aboriginal Wisdom*, the ancient ones speak of the necessity for finishing, or bringing closure to, our unfinished business with others. Until we do, we will remain energetically tied. In the ancient Hawaiian healing tradition called Ho'Oponopono, the ancients suggest that when we have experienced hurt with another we say, "I'm sorry, forgive me, thank you, I love you."[8] And, I like to add, "May we both be happy. May we both be free." The practice stresses not to try and figure it out but rather to feel and express the intention to be healed, to forgive ourselves and others and, as a result, to better release the ties that bind. Hindus believe that such hurt or angst with another is both the expression of and the result of karma, or in some measure a reaping of what we have sown. To be free, we must acknowledge and accept responsibility for our part and, as a result, a deeper truth, or dharma, may be revealed. The Buddha reminded us, "If you truly loved yourself you could never hurt another."[9] This is a remembrance that what we carry for another, be it hate or love, is automatically recorded on and felt in our

6. Errico, *Setting a Trap*, 89.
7. Errico, *Setting a Trap*, 91.
8. Bodin and Lamboy, *Book of Ho'oponopono*, 2.
9. Deltour, *Buddhist Quotes*, 52.

own heart. And from a more contemporary source, Joan Borysenko, in her book *Mending the Mind; Minding the Body*, suggests we reflect upon our difficult relationships with others by asking the following question, "Would you rather be right or would you rather be happy?"[10]

In these two lines of the prayer, we approach a very similar intention. We seek to become released, or untied, as we recognize that what is occurring inwardly is instantly occurring outwardly. Yet, whether we are working on forgiving ourselves or others, it is important to remember that, for most of us, forgiveness is not a happening. It's a process. It is very important not to gloss over our deep wounds with spiritual platitudes or with positive escapism. This is why it is often recommended that we practice the art of self—and other—forgiveness regularly if we are to return to a sense of wholeness and inner peace. Acknowledging this, we realize we may have to enter the deep caverns of our heart many times to gently peel away the layers of hurt, anger, and resentment to truly be able to release those ties that bind us to others.

The journey to forgiveness surely begins with us first, for only then can we authentically offer our forgiveness to others. And it takes much courage to enter the very caves we may have for so long avoided but there, right there, we find the very treasure we are seeking, the gift of freedom. This realization is beautifully expressed by the image of the lotus flower that grows from the muck to blossom above the water. In other words it, like we, blossom, not *in spite of*, but, rather, *because of*. When it comes to our humble, human, walk with our God, *this* is the truth that sets us free. And, it is also lovingly expressed in the *Gospel of Thomas*, when Jesus said, "When you give rise to that

10. Borysenko, *Mending the Mind*, 149.

which is within you, what you have will save you. If you do not give rise to it, what you do not have will destroy you.[11]

Here are some other reminders from Jesus about forgiveness:

Biblical References:

> Matt 6: 14-15: "For if ye forgive men their trespasses, your heavenly Father will also forgive you: But if ye forgive not men their trespasses, neither will your Father forgive your trespasses."

> Luke 6: 37: "Judge not, and ye shall not be judged: Condemn not, and ye shall not be condemned: forgive, and ye shall be forgiven."

> Luke 23: 34: "Father, forgive them; for they know not what they do."

Questions for Reflection

1. Reflect upon how you have thought about the process of forgiveness in the past. How does your previous way relate to the way expressed here in the Aramaic?

2. Can you imagine a situation, in your opinion, in which you would find great difficulty, or, in fact, would *not* feel compelled to forgive?

3. Reflect upon how "forgiveness" relates to "justice."

4. Whom, or what, are you in the process of forgiving?

---

11. Davies, trans., *Gospel of Thomas*, 76.

Wela tahlan l'nesyuna
And lead us not into temptation
Resist Forgetfulness . . .

ela patzan min bisha
but deliver us from evil
Cultivate Harmony . . .

HAVING REMEMBERED TO *embrace fullness* and to *forgive ourself and others,* we are now ready to approach, perhaps, the most challenging aspect of our daily existence—what to do with temptation and evil.

Aramaic Translations:

Neil Douglas-Klotz:
Wela tahlan: "'don't let us enter' or 'don't let us be seduced by the appearance of.'"[1]
l'nesyuna: "'temptation' . . . but also points to 'forgetfulness' or 'losing of oneself in appearances.'"[2]

---

1. Douglas-Klotz, *Prayers of the Cosmos*, 35.
2. Douglas-Klotz, *Prayers of the Cosmos*, 35.

[*ela*] *patzan*: "loosen the hold of, give liberty from, or break the seal that binds us to."[3]

[*min*] *bisha*: "evil" or "error," but in the Aramaic also points to a sense of being "unripe" or engaging in "inappropriate action."[4]

Rocco A. Errico:

[As with the previous two lines, Errico begins with a translation of the full line—yet, here, is also a breakdown by word.]

Wla ta-alan l'nisyona ella pasan min beesha: "'And do not let us enter into temptation, but deliver us from evil (error).' . . . The idea being to 'keep me out of trouble' or 'prevent me from entering harmful circumstances.'"[5]

ta-alan: "derived from the Aramaic root *al* . . . meaning 'to enter, to attack, to fight, to wrestle, to contend.'"[6] Referencing Matt 26:41, pointing to forgetfulness, "Wake up and pray, that you may not enter (*ta-alon*) into temptation."[7]

l'nisyona: "tests, trials, temptations . . . can also connote materialism or worldliness."[8]

[ella] *pasan*: "'part us, separate us, set us free' . . . from erroneous thinking and actions that lead us into more problems and evils."[9]

[min] *beesha*: "'evil,' . . . from the root *beesha*, to err, to displease, to harm, to be evil, to seem bad, to mistake, to afflict, to be unripe, to be immature, and to be unfortunate."[10]

---

3. Douglas-Klotz, *Prayers of the Cosmos*, 35.
4. Douglas-Klotz, *Prayers of the Cosmos*, 35.
5. Errico, *Setting a Trap*, 99.
6. Errico, *Setting a Trap*, 101.
7. Errico, *Setting a Trap*, 102.
8. Errico, *Setting a Trap*, 102.
9. Errico, *Setting a Trap*, 103.
10. Errico, *Setting a Trap*, 103.

> Errico ends affirming, "Only God—the true, good, inherent spiritual power who is a living part of us all—can direct and separate us from evil or mistakes."[11]

Neil Douglas-Klotz begins his translation asserting that these lines are, perhaps, the least understood and mistranslated lines in the prayer. I could not agree more. The misunderstanding appears to begin with the first part of this line. Both Douglas-Koltz and Errico translate *Wela tahlan* to mean, "don't let us enter into," as opposed to the current English translation, "lead us not." And both surmise that *l'nesyuna*, temptation, points to forgetfulness and the possibility of losing oneself in appearances leading to unwanted tests, trials and temptations.

Let's look closer. That *Wela tahlan* is best translated in the Aramaic as, "don't let us enter into," as opposed to the English translation, "lead us not," feels in complete harmony with the *Abwoon d'bwashmaya*, and the remembrance that there is no separation between us and our creator. So, clearly, if there is no one outside of ourselves, there is no one who could lead us anywhere—least of all God. And, if we remember that God is within our very breath, breathing us each moment into the remembrance of our unity with all, to where could we possibly be led? No, instead, we pray here for guidance, to not be allowed to enter into *l'nesyuna*, temptation, caused by forgetfulness, whereby we become focused on outer changing, worldly circumstances instead of on our inner, innate, eternal fullness. This is beautifully expressed by Rumi using "sleep" as a metaphor for forgetfulness: "The breeze at dawn has secrets to tell you. Don't go back to sleep! You must ask for what you really want. Don't go back to sleep! People are going back

---

11. Errico, *Setting a Trap*, 106.

and forth across the doorsill where the two worlds touch. The door is round and open. Don't go back to sleep!"[12]

"Forgetfulness" is a key word here because we cannot "forget" something we don't already know! How often during the day, day after day, do we "forget," fall into our ego fears and feel lost. How very sweet it is to know that we can wake up or "remember" who it is we are, a child of God, made in his image (see Gen 1:27), a spiritual being having a human experience as some have described. In moments of wakefulness, recalling again that here, in our creator's great creation, all is transitory, meaning that all we experience is born, lives and is transformed, including our bodies, beliefs and emotions. Only the soul, the divine spark of our creator within, who loved us into birth, is eternal.

And, from what are we asking to be delivered from as a result of our waking up? How comforting to know that, while *min bisha* does mean evil, both Douglas-Klotz and Errico write that it also points to a sense of being unripe. I would offer that, when we are in tune with our breath and walk, in rhythm with our inner divinity, our words and actions are naturally ripe for the moment. In such circumstances, synchronicity abounds and we experience being carried along by our beloved creator who breaths us into life each moment. In those times when we may be unripe for the moment, we may feel out of sync, have temporarily fallen asleep and may experience separation, fear or loss in our emotional desert. In our fast-paced world, being out of rhythm can lead to burnout, fatigue, even illness.

While many of us may have difficulty with the notion that some part of us may be evil, most of us can relate to this feeling of separation or un-ripeness. It is why many faith traditions say that at the core of our greatest fear is

12. Barks and Green, *Illuminated Prayer*, 48.

the belief that we are alone, separate, and not connected to, or a part of, any cosmic plan—that we are, instead, simply floundering about without aim or purpose. This is, perhaps, for most of us, a more applicable translation of "evil."

· But perhaps the most innate experience of our ripeness, as opposed to un-ripeness, comes in the expression of what I previously described as our unique note, the impulse that moves us toward wholeness, our sacred duty, role or purpose. When we are responding to this impulse, we may experience joy and success or challenge and struggle but, when following our inner note, harmony becomes the goal instead of a particular preconceived outcome. From this perspective, our struggles provide rich compost from which to grow and flower deeper and more beautiful creations. Here, we are not just delivered from entering into forgetfulness but we are flowering in the full expression of our divinity, as instruments of the living God. Here *we* do not sing our note. Rather, our note is gracefully and delightfully sung by our creator through us. This I would offer is the antithesis of evil. In waking up, we see clearly. We are here, in heaven, on earth.

And here, in heaven, our breath finds deep peace. Our walk finds harmony with our surroundings. Synchronicity abounds as we become the hollow flute for the most appropriate action in each circumstance. We don't have to worry anymore about doing something "right" for we have fallen right with our God. Rhythm carries us. Breath sustains us. And, in those sweet moments, joy becomes us.

Enjoy these additional pearls of wisdom.

Biblical References:

Job 8:11–13: "Can the rush grow up without mire? Can the flag grow without water? Whilst it is yet in his greenness, and not cut down, it withereth before any other herb. So are the paths of all that forget God."

Ps 103:1–2: "Bless the Lord, O my soul: and all that is within me, bless his holy name. Bless the Lord, O my soul, and forget not all his benefits."

Matt 7:17 and Matt 7:20: "Even so every good [ripe] tree bringeth forth good [ripe] fruit; but a corrupt [unripe] tree bringeth forth evil [unripe] fruit. [Matt 7:20] Wherefore by their fruits ye shall know them."

Eccl 3: 1: "To everything there is a season, and a time to every purpose under heaven."

Questions for Reflection

1. What are the forces in your life that cause you to forget or fall asleep? What might you do, recommit to, in order to cultivate a ripe place within for remembrance?

2. Recall a time, activity or occurrence when you felt in complete harmony with your creator, when you were carried by the rhythm of your breath and bathed in peace, regardless of outer circumstances.

3. For what are you, currently, cultivating ripeness?

Metol dilakhie malkutha
For thine is the kingdom
For Thine is the Vision . . .

wahayla, wateshbukhta
and the power, and the glory
the Energy . . . and the Song . . .

l'ahlam almin.
forever

Ameyn.
Amen

HERE WE SEE THE ending of the prayer as recorded in Matt 6: 9–13. This ending is not included with the prayer as recorded in Luke 11:1–4. While scholars do not agree whether this line was an original part of the prayer, most do agree that some kind of closing would have been rendered to summarize the specific suggestions Jesus was offering to instruct those present how to pray. In addition, these final lines do summarize beautifully the major themes of the prayer and, in fact, return us to the beginning again, in circular fashion, ending as we began with the *ahhhh* sound.

Aramaic Translations:

Neil Douglas-Klotz:

[Metol] *dilakhie*: "'For thine is the kingdom' . . . also shows another planting image: a field fertile and abundant, one sufficient to produce everything."[1] Douglas-Klotz also refers to the "return to the creative visioning of God, the power to accomplish these visions and the beauty that adds grace and artistry to them."[2]

malkutha: recalls the "I can" in the line, *Teytey malkuthakh*, or "royalty that permeates the entire universe."[3]

[wa]*hayla*: "life force or energy that produces and sustains . . . not 'power over' but power in unison with all natural creation."[4]

[wa]*teshbukhta*: "glory . . . but also calls forth more exactly the image of a 'song'—a glorious harmony returning divine light and sound to matter in equilibrium. The roots of the word also present the picture of a 'generative fire that leads to astonishment.'"[5]

---

1. Douglas-Klotz, *Prayers of the Cosmos*, 38.
2. Douglas-Klotz, *Prayers of the Cosmos*, 38.
3. Douglas-Klotz, *Prayers of the Cosmos*, 38.
4. Douglas-Klotz, *Prayers of the Cosmos*, 38.
5. Douglas-Klotz, *Prayers of the Cosmos*, 38.

l'ahlam almin: "age to age . . . for ever and ever . . . from gathering to gathering"[6]

Ameyn: "'Amen' . . . sealed agreements . . . a solemn oath."[7]

Rocco A. Errico:

[Consistent with the commentary for this second half of the prayer, Errico begins with a translation of the full line—yet, here, as with the previous line, is also a breakdown by word.]

Mitol ddeelakhee malkutha whaila wtishbohta: la-alam almeen. Amen: "Because the kingdom, the power and the glory belong to You: from all ages throughout all the ages. Amen. One may also translate the verse to read: 'Yours are the kingdom (counsel), energy, song, and praise throughout all the ages. Sealed in faith, trust, and truth.'"[8]

[*Metal ddeelakhee malkutha*] [w]*haila*: "'power' . . . also denotes might, energy, force, potency and strength."[9]

[w]*tishbohta*: "glory, praise, honor, and magnificence. . . . Liturgically, it refers to song, hymn or chant. . . . Its Aramaic root *shwh* denotes to praise, to glorify, to honor, to magnify, and to celebrate."[10]

la-alam almeen: "'from all ages, throughout all the ages,' . . . Others translate the phrase as 'world without end.'"[11]

Amen. "'to make firm' . . . to declare that we will 'back up and stand by what we have just

---

6. Douglas-Klotz, *Prayers of the Cosmos*, 38.

7. Douglas-Klotz, *Prayers of the Cosmos*, 38.

8. Errico, *Setting a Trap*, 109.

9. Errico, *Setting a Trap*, 111.

10. Errico, *Setting a Trap*, 111–12.

11. Errico, *Setting a Trap*, 110.

prayed. We will be faithful to our commitment in prayer.'"[12]

Jesus summarized the core message for each of us in this line of the prayer:

Metol dilakhie malkutha: **For Thine is the [kingdom] Vision**: *Thine* means *us* as children of the living God made in his image . . . and we are seeded with the creative "I Can!" to bring forth our unique vision, our expression of God's kingdom here on earth, in service to the greater good, with passion and joy!

wahayla: **the [power] Energy**: We are breathed into life by the divine life force of our creator and, so breathed, are in constant unison with all the energy we need to bring forth our unique expressions of God!

wateshbukhta: **and the [glory] Song:** And, in those sweet moments of remembrance, we become the song and the entire cosmos dances in glory!

l'ahlam almin. Ahhh-meyn: **forever. Amen**. And, we stand before God to make our committed, faithful oath.

Biblical References:

> Luke 12:32: "Fear not little flock; for it is your Father's good pleasure to give you the kingdom."

> John 1:12: "But as many as received him, to them gave he power to become the sons of God."

> John 11:40: "Said I not unto thee, that, if thou wouldest believe, thou shouldest see the glory of God?"

---

12. Errico, *Setting a Trap*, 114.

Questions for Reflection

1. Do you have a sense of what your personal vision, in God's great plan, here in his kingdom on earth, might look like?

2. What does the realization that we have all the energy we need to bring forth our vision, or divine purpose, say to you?

3. There is an African tradition that would create a song for a child when he or she is born. This "song" would then be repeated at all the important transitions and events in the child's life. How might it relate to our unique song in this context?

4. Reflect in your own words how this last line both summarizes and brings to life, full circle, the major themes of the prayer.

Conclusion

AND SO, COMING FULL circle, we have found ourselves at the beginning, now fully cognizant of ourselves as children of the living God, and, as such, like the prayer, a world without end (see Isa 45:17). Let's take a look:

> With *Abwoon d'bwashmaya*, we **remember** our innate connection with our creator. Remembering, we naturally turn inward to **create space**, *nethqadash shmakh*, for the clearing of our inner field to receive the seeds of divine guidance. Receiving divine guidance, we **align with the creator**, *tey tey malkutha*, to engage in harmonious action making God's will our will. We are now poised to **manifest the vision** and **become heaven on earth**, *nehwey tzevyanach aykana d'bwashmaya aph b'arha*.
>
> In our daily walk with others, we seek to **embrace fullness**, *hawvlan lachma d'sunqanan yaomana*, to **forgive our self and forgive others**, *washboqlan khaubayn (wakhtahayn) aykana daph khnan shbwoqan l'khayyabayn*, and to stay awake to our eternal nature as we **resist forgetfulness** and seek to **cultivate harmony**, *wela tahlan l'nesyuna, ela patzan min bisha*. And, in such moments of remembering our innate connection with our creator, we become aligned with God's kingdom or vision for us, **for thine is the vision**, *metol dilakhie malkutha*, experience all the natural laws of the universe supplying the

power, ***the energy***, *wahayla*, and we become ***the song***, *wateshbukhta*, as our ecstatic cry rings out in glory!

Such a realization belongs to us just as our creator's breath belongs to us and is our birthright just as all children carry the birthright of our divine creator. This realization is not something we have to ask for but, rather, is something waiting within each of us to simply receive. This is what it means to pray!

And, all there is left to say is . . .

Amen

How the Lord's Prayer *Informs Our Understanding of the Cross*

THE IMAGE OF THE cross is one that elicits strong emotions for many. It's hard to see an image of the cross without imagining the one called Jesus hanging there. Such an image is so stark that it remains personal to the story of the resurrection for many of us. Yet, I would offer that, if we can look with soft eyes, we may see beyond the traditional story to a most blessed message waiting to inform our everyday lives.

If we consider the vertical part of the cross to represent our innate connection with our creator and the horizontal part to represent our experience in the world of physicality, we can see *Abwoon d'bwashmaya* right in front of us. Moreover, Jesus suffered. Is this not true for us as well? Yet, Jesus could withstand all the world's suffering on the horizontal plane because he *knew to whom he belonged* on the vertical plane. *Here,* I would offer, lies the critical message Jesus so lovingly portrayed for us through his suffering, dying and, finally, in his resurrection.

As he taught those who would hear, he knew the kingdom was within, *nethqadash shmakh*, so aligning to receive counsel and do the will of his creator, *teytey malkuthak*, allowed him to endure all and complete his sacred duty for all humanity. In his surrender to what was to unfold, he beautifully demonstrated *nehwey sebyanach aykanna d'bwashmaya aph b'arha*, or how to be heaven on earth even in the most trying of circumstances. He became the living example of *you can endure all the suffering the world has to offer when you know to whom you belong. Knowing, you can remember that your body, and all that is endured here, will pass away but "you," as a child of God, will not. You, as a unique expression of the creator, are eternal.* Truly, this realization naturally creates a deep yearning to pray, to be connected to our Lord who breathed us into life, sustains us, and will bring us home. Like Jesus, we want to experience that which is eternal within us. We want God.

And, Jesus *lived* the second half of the prayer as he *died* on the cross. He knew he had all he needed within for transcending death, *hawvlan lachma d'sunqanan yaomana*, and even asked for those who had trespassed against him to be forgiven, *washboqlan khaubayn (wakhtahayn) aykana daph khnan shbwoqan l'khayyabayn*. One could say that, perhaps, in the most painful moments just before physical death, Jesus had a moment of forgetfulness, *l'nesyuna*, when he cried out, "My God, My God, why hast thou forsaken me?" (Matt 27:46). Yet, it appears he was soon able to free himself from such erroneous thinking, *ela patzan min bisha*, as Matt 27:50 tells us, "when he had cried again with a loud voice, yielded up the ghost," surrendering into the inevitable journey home to his creator.

In his living and his dying, Jesus demonstrated how to make our walk on the earth a holy, breathing prayer. He dared to tell those who would hear that they had the kingdom, the *malkutha*, within, and that being in constant unison with the life force of their creator, *wahayla*, they had all the power they needed to become heaven on earth, and, to ultimately, express the glory, *wateshbukta*, the ecstatic cry!

> All around us we have known you.
> All creation lives to hold you.
> In our living and our dying,
> we are bringing you to birth.
>
> "God Beyond All Names"[1]

---

1. Farrell, "God Beyond All Names."

Sampling of Participants' Lord's Prayers

SINCE 2012, WHEN THE first edition of this book was published, I have given numerous classes, workshops, and presentations on the Lord's Prayer in Aramaic. In the class format, which allows for the beginning of in-depth study, ideally a minimum of eight to twelve weeks is required. Each week, participants are encouraged to take a line of the prayer into their spiritual practice and to reflect upon how the essence of the line informs their daily lives. At the end of the study, participants are invited to write their own personal versions of the prayer, reflecting their expanded understanding, provided by both the study and the practice of the prayer in Aramaic. Again and again, participants have reported that learning to recite the prayer in Aramaic breathed new life into the familiar English words, broadened their understanding of what Jesus was really saying, and allowed for a fuller expression of the prayer in their lives. Below is just a sampling of prayers participants have written over the years.

SAMPLING OF PARTICIPANTS' LORD'S PRAYERS

Julie's Prayer

Oh Divine Creator

With every breathe I take I remember the kingdom of heaven is within me

My heart is open

Come

Come fill me and satiate my desire for YOU

As I wholly surrender to Thy will

Make me an instrument of YOUR peace so that I may be heaven on earth

Grant me the understanding to recognize all I need in my daily life

Release the bonds that I have with others whose personal boundaries I have crossed

And help me forgive those who have caused me hurt

Guide me to be nonjudgmental

And deliver me from the darkness of being out of harmony with YOU

For everything I need is within me when I embrace YOU

For YOU sustain me

With a sweet, soulful, and harmonious heart-song

Again and again

Amen

—JULIE BEAUCHEMIN

Anne's Prayer

My dear Lord from whom all life, light and love is manifest, I honor and praise your name and your spirit that dwells within me and within all of your creation.

Your kingdom is of great beauty and is in all that is seen and unseen.

I pray that you will be made known to me and that I will listen and follow as I walk in communion with you and others.

Thank you for forgiving me for all my faults and failures and for cleansing me of all guilt. In Your Name and with your grace I forgive myself and others.

Thank you for protecting and freeing me from all that keeps me from my purpose and for the knowledge and strength to do all things that are right and holy.

I know that there is nothing impossible with you my Lord, my God.

Amen

—Anne Hebert

John's Prayer

Remember where you have come from.
Open your heart to me, your Creator
And align yourself to my vibration and sound.
Surrender and be the image of me,
Reflecting my joy within you.
Remember your kinship to all of creation.
Forgive yourself,
Then forgive others.
Remember always that I am here for you,

SAMPLING OF PARTICIPANTS' LORD'S PRAYERS

As my spirit within you abounds.
This is my vision for you.
I have given you life, now give sound to my song.
Forever and ever.
Amen

—JOHN SILVA

Winnie's Prayer

Creator of all, it is in the breathing of the wind, the silence of the falling snow, the sound of the water caressing the shoreline, the glint of the sun's rays filtering through the trees, and the darkness of the night sky interrupted only by twinkling stars that I see you, hear you, feel you, know you, remember and experience Oneness. Soften the walls of my heart, allowing it to swell like the ever-widening, all-encompassing, circular ripples on a pond, creating a sacred space within me where we meet. Align my Divine glowing ember with the warmth of Your blazing fire illuminating the path that I am to follow and igniting my vision. Place my feet firmly on the ground that I might move forward with confidence and conviction; passionately fulfilling my life's purpose. Nourish me mentally, physically, emotionally and spiritually, daily and from moment to moment along the way, that I might be of the greatest service to You. Lighten the load that I carry on my shoulders: mistaken beliefs, inner shames, failures, frustrations, all things that do not serve me; as I release the burden of falsehoods that I have carried for others. May I walk in Your footsteps, keeping pace, staying in the rhythm of Your stride, and singing harmony to our song. You have blessed me with vision that needs no eyes, a river of energy to fulfill my life's purpose, and an inner place that knows unity; may it be so from lifetime to lifetime. May the strength of these statements form the solid ground upon which I walk. Amen

—WINNIE ROBICHAUD

Sue's Prayer

O Great Beloved One who in each moment breathes me

Help me clear a space to gratefully live a holy life in your name

Align my will with Your Divine Will for me

May Your Divine Love be manifested through my earthly life to all creation

Thank You for Your daily banquet offering of bread and practical understanding

Help me untie the knots connecting me to others, as I release my angst toward them

Keep me from falling into the illusion of earthly life

Free me from what holds me back, so I can walk Your path with Joy!

From You comes my vision, energy, and song

Which unites us all throughout all the Ages

FOREVER

Amen

—SUE HILLS

SAMPLING OF PARTICIPANTS' LORD'S PRAYERS

Jan's Prayer

Oh, Intangible Unified Mystery; Source and Bearer of all Creation

I am emptied to embrace your Illuminated Song.

May your Empowered Vision sacredly play through me.

Let the Song begin, I welcome it wholeheartedly that I may walk in Harmony and be recognized as One Who Sings from the Place where Heaven and Earth meet!

Remind me in each illuminated moment that

I *am* enough, *have* enough and that there is sufficient support to fulfill my earthly purpose.

Let me release all tangled threads and rigid knots harbored within that I may forgive myself, thus others, and allow for the unencumbered Sacred flow through me.

Oh, don't let me fall into forgetfulness, left to wallow in false illusion! May the bond that distracts me from my purpose be broken that "I" may once again sing in cosmic harmony. Allow for my ripening in its own, sweet time.

For in this Mystery lies the full potential of All, the One Glorious, Universal Song, as it was, as it is now and as it shall be sung for all the ages.

From this empowered place of Unity and Harmony, I say,

"Be it so."

—JAN GROSSMAN

Lucille's Prayer

God, Our heavenly Father, may your name be kept holy.

May your kingdom in heaven and on earth bring peace and harmony to all its inhabitants.

Forgive us the wrongs that we have done that we may forgive others.

Help us to do only what is right. Forgive those who do not believe in your love.

Protect those who are lost.

God—You are the kingdom of heaven.

The kingdom, power, and praise belong to you forever.

Amen

—Lucille Thonis

Kathie's Prayer

Loving and gentle father of all creation,

You are the source of all goodness, grace and compassion.

You have breathed life into us and are within our hearts; a part of us.

We must remember; the source of our wholeness; the source of our oneness;

Our connection to you.

Through every sound, light and vibration, we remember our sacred unity.

SAMPLING OF PARTICIPANTS' LORD'S PRAYERS

We ask that our hearts open and our thoughts and desires align to your divine will.

We seek your guidance;

Listening in the silence to rediscover our true selves and our true purpose.

Separation from you brings loneliness and yearning.

Forgetting our essence furthers our distance from you.

We sink into the rhythm of the breath and we remember.

We feel whole.

We remember to whom we belong.

—Kathie Thonis

Karen's Prayer

I may walk through the most barren of lands, but oh Abba you are here. Waiting for me.

I shall gently plow away layers of earthly soil to make space for your presence. A divine presence which is beyond my understanding and yet closer to me than I am to myself.

Bring forth the glorious "I can" making manifest the potential that quivers in this seed.

See it break forth and grow; the stem commits and aligns with you while the earth rises up in support.

Oh Spectacle, it is a field of lily's all bursting forth.

Abba of all, sustain us, feed us, quench our thirst with your holy lessons.

Unburden those I have faulted, as I untie the knots of those who crossed my boundaries.

Keep us awake to the truth so that we may be ripe and in tune with holy unity.

From you comes the Farmers Field where the "I can" grows and matures into your vision and song from gathering to gathering.

Amen

—Karen Hews

Beth's Prayer

Oh Great Spirit, creator of the Universe and all her creatures,

I am open and I am listening.

May Thy will be my will.

May I be of service, finding power through

peace, and strength through service.

Live through me and make manifest Thy will

through my words and deeds.

I humbly offer my life in service to the good of all.

I agree to my place in the world of women and

men, in the world of people and things.

Help me to know that the world is infinitely abundant and benevolent,

And that I have always had all that I need,

So that I may forgive all perceived injustice

within myself and the world.

Help me to remember the truth of life, love,

beauty, and our divine existence,

and to resist the forgetfulness of darkness.

May the blessings of your light, your glory, and

your infinite love and grace

shine and express through me in all that I bring to the world,

that my life may be of benefit to all beings, now and forever more.

Amen.

—Beth Cohen

Ilona's Prayer

Our Creator which art in all,
precious is your grace.
We give thanks for the space
to express all that you caress
with love unbounded.

May all we say and do
be true to you,

with no illusion or confusion,
here and there, and everywhere.
And as we of your bounty share,
we ask only for enough
so that our song may rise up above
. . . loud and strong.
We belong
to the whole and the whole is in us,
so to forgive and be forgiven is one and the same . . .
it is from one divine source that we came.

When in our humanness we forget and stray,
help us again to find the way
to the core of our being,
where peace and joy await,
for in your time, it is never too late
to truly listen and submit to your voice
. . . the gift of a joyous choice.
May your eternal spirit continue to inspire us to dream,
To live life to the fullest in your stream
of Love
. . . and to sing and dance forever in harmony
with all creation. Amen.

—Ilona Kwiecien

Carrie's Prayer

Always Divine, Always Connected,
I lay palm fronds to prepare my path so my holiness can shine forth.
I align with my deep divinity—truth is truth.

SAMPLING OF PARTICIPANTS' LORD'S PRAYERS

My vision is supported and will manifest on
earth as it already is by the divine.

I am filled with all the understanding, all the resources,
in every moment, for full illumination.

I forgive myself any wrongs I have done to myself or
others; likewise,

I forgive others any wrongs they have done to me or
others.

I am awake; I will not be unskillful.

I am full of my vision; I have the energy and will sing
my song.

This I covenant with myself, My Divine Self, my class
and all beings.

Amen.

—Carrie Ives

Richard's Prayer

Remember that God gave birth, through breath,
to a self-perpetuating creation.

Make space in your psyche for recollection—a
personal cosmological paradigm shift.

Then you will know your place and responsibility in it all.

And your worldview will emerge as incarnate,
in this lifetime.

But the space-making is a process and includes a daily diet of spiritual nourishment, and a practice of boldly walking, with love, through in the midst of the surrounding dark antithesis of creation, forgiving to be forgiven. In addition, commit to avoiding all arising tempters of forgetfulness, any way you can.

For you have always known, deep down, that you are, and always have been, a part of this God-breathed self-perpetuating creation.

Commit yourself to this reality, as I have.

JESUS

—RICHARD D. LAKE

Rhonda's Prayer

Oh Divine Creator of all that is above and below

I'm humbled by your amazing grace, which fills the wounded spaces

Your unconditional love breathes my Soul

Which offers "Holiness" wholeness

And thus provides pure alignment of mind, body and spirit to your will Father

So I may allow the beauty of heavens creation on earth be fulfilled

Your sacred sustenance lord is my infinite divine supply

Forgive me of what I have not seen or understood

And, may I offer the same to my beloved brothers and sisters

Lead, guide and direct me lord on the path of goodness

And awaken me from separateness and fear

SAMPLING OF PARTICIPANTS' LORD'S PRAYERS

To instill your vision

Of your majestic creative forces that wrote our song

Forever

Amen

—Rhonda Schienle

Bill's Prayer

Remember our continuous connection to Father-Mother God.

Sacred is thy Name's universal Divine vibration.

Align all of me with the Creator ("not my will, but thine"). Manifest Divine Will always. Make me an instrument of Heaven on Earth.

Give us this day, remember our daily Divine Illumination! Purify me and dissolve the residues of karmic debt. As we forgive and release others who have acted against us.

Lead us from forgetfulness to constant diligence in always seeking harmony with Divine Will. May we unite with Father-Mother God's creation in Dharmic Sovereignty, through alignment with primordial Divine Will which enables all power, all order and all glory in this Song of creation. Forever.

Amen.

—Bill Francis Barry

Stephanie's Prayer

With each breath, I remember my connection to the One who breathes me into life each moment.

I quiet an inner space to listen. I hear the hallowed call of my name and I answer.

Oh Beloved, align my will with Thy will to serve Your purpose for my life.

I pray heaven be brought to earth through me.

Satiated me with Your Love.

Release me from the ties that bind as I seek to forgive myself and others.

Keep me awake to Your Beauty and help me to ripen in Your time. And, when darkness comes, cradle me in Your Grace so I may blossom, not in spite of, but, because of.

For You have seeded the vision for my life within each breath I take.

You fill me anew each moment with all I need to bring forth Your Love.

You have made me an instrument of your Holy Song.

And, I, in gratitude overflowing, can only sing...

Amen

—Stephanie Rutt

Bibliography

Artson, Bradley Shavit. "Holy, Holy, Holy! Jewish Affirmations of Panentheism." In *Panentheism across the World's Traditions*, edited by Loriliai Biernacki and Philip Clayton, 18–36. New York: Oxford University Press, 2014.

Barks, Coleman, and Michael Green, eds. *The Illuminated Prayer: The Five Times Prayer of the Sufis*. New York: Random House, 2000.

Bodin, Luc, and Nathalie Boden Lamboy. *The Book of Ho'oponopono: The Hawaiian Practice for Forgiveness and Healing*. Rochester, VT: Destiny, 2012.

Borysenko, Joan. *Mending the Mind: Minding the Body*. Cambridge, MA: Da Capo, 2007.

Davies, Stevan, trans. *The Gospel of Thomas*. Boston: Shambhala Library, 2004.

Deltour, Frederic, ed. *Buddhist Quotes: Meditation, Happiness, Inner Peace*. N.p.: Frederic Deltour, 2016.

Dhar, Abu, trans. "110 Hadith Qudsi." *The Hadith Library*. http://ahadith.co.uk/chapter.php?cid=144.

Douglas-Klotz. *Prayers of the Cosmos: Meditations on the Aramaic Words of Jesus*. New York: HarperCollins, 1990.

Errico, Rocco A. *Setting a Trap for God: The Aramaic Prayer of Jesus*. Unity Village, MO: Unity House, 1997.

Farrell, Bernadette. "God Beyond All Names." Track 4 on *God Beyond All Names*. Compact disc. St. Thomas More Group & Frank Brownstead, 1991.

———. "O God You Search Me." Track 5 on *Christ Be Our Light*. Compact disc. OCP, 1994.

Fox, Matthew, ed. *Meditations with Meister Eckhart*. Rochester, VT: Bear, 1983.

Johnson, E. A. *Quest for the Living God: Mapping Frontiers in the Theology of God*. New York: Continuum, 2007.

Kabir. *The Bijak of Kabir*. Translated by Linda Hass and Shukdeo Singh. New York: Oxford University Press, 2002.

BIBLIOGRAPHY

Kornfield, Jack. *A Path with Heart: A Guide through the Perils and Promises of Spiritual Life.* New York: Bantam, 1993.

Mitchell, Stephen, trans. *The Tao Te Ching.* https://taoteching.org.uk/.

Mother Teresa. *In the Heart of the World: Thoughts, Stories and Prayers.* Edited by Becky Benenate. Novato, CA: New World Library, 1997.

Spong, John Shelby. *The Sins of Scripture: Exposing the Bible's Texts of Hate to Reveal the God of Love.* San Francisco: HarperCollins, 2005.

Satchidananda, Sri Swami. *The Living Gita: The Complete Bhagavad Gita and Commentary.* New York: Holt, 1988.

Scherman, Nosson, and Meir Zlotowitz, eds. *Tehillim: The Book of Psalms with an Interlinear Translation.* New York: Mesorah, 2013.

Schutte, Dan. "All One People." Track 9 on *Drawn by a Dream.* Compact disc. Oregon Catholic Press, 2013.

Therese of Lisieux. *The Poetry of Saint Therese of Lisieux.* Translated by Donald Kinney. Washington, DC: ICS, 1996.

www.ingramcontent.com/pod-product-compliance
Lightning Source LLC
Chambersburg PA
CBHW070325100426
42743CB00011B/2560